Crime
in
Time

Robert Gott

HORWITZ
MARTIN

HORWITZ MARTIN

Horwitz Martin Education
A Division of Horwitz
  Publications Pty Ltd
55 Chandos St
St Leonards NSW 2065
Australia

Horwitz Martin Education
Unit 15, Cressex Enterprise Centre
Lincoln Road
High Wycombe, Bucks HP12 3RL
United Kingdom

a black dog book
Designed by Josie Semmler
Cover photo by John Brash. Digital composition by Josie Semmler.
Illustrations by Peter Mather, pp. 3, 5, 33, 47, 49, 63, 65, 73, 76.
The editor would like to thank the following for permission to
reproduce images: Felicity Hill, p. 26; Old Melbourne Gaol, p. 27;
Queensland Police Force, pp. 67, 68, 69. Other images are from the
editor's, author's and designer's collections or are in the public
domain. Every effort has been made to contact original sources,
where known, for permissions. If an infringement has
inadvertently occurred, the editor wishes to apologise. The
publisher and editor would like to thank Garry Chapman and
Vicki Hazell, the educational consultants for the series.

National Library of Australia
Cataloguing information
Gott, Robert.
  Crime in time.

ISBN 0 7253 1660 8

1. Criminal investigation - Juvenile literature. 2. Crime - Juvenile
literature. 3. Criminal investigation - History - Juvenile literature.
I. Title. (Series: Phenomena).

364.1

Printed and bound in Australia by
Sands Print Group Limited
2 3 4 5
00 01 02

Understanding the Horwitz Martin logo

Thoth
The Egyptian
god of wisdom,
mathematics and writing.

Contents

Introduction

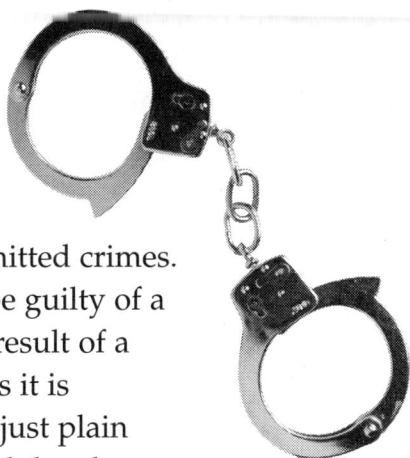

PEOPLE have always committed crimes. One day even you may be guilty of a crime. Sometimes crime is a result of a desire for revenge, sometimes it is because of greed or anger or just plain hatred. Sometimes people feel they have to break laws to survive. Perhaps they are hungry, or cold, or in danger.

Some of the crimes people commit are bizarre. Some murderers even discover that killing a person isn't as easy as they thought. Not too long ago, a wife who was angry with her husband, drugged him and hired someone to shoot him. The assassin shot him in the head. This didn't kill him so she hired someone else to shoot him through the heart. This didn't work either. He recovered fully and even forgave his wife. Sometimes the way people behave and the crimes they

commit are a phenomenon beyond reasonable explanation. What we have said is a crime has changed over time, as have the way we deal with criminals. Gruesome public executions were once common. The ways in which we investigate crimes have changed too. Evidence is now more important than superstition. Once, if a woman kept a cat, this was proof enough that she was a witch. Imagine that. The family cat curled up on your lap might have won you a ticket to a public spectacle—with you being burned alive as the entertainment.

chapter 1
What is a Crime?

Imagine...

"MY FATHER? I never met him. He took off before I was born. Mum was seven months pregnant. She reckoned he was a total loser. Can I have a smoke?"

The detective interviewing the girl who said this leaned back in his chair, put his hands behind his head and said, "No. There's no smoking in the interview room. Besides you're 13 years old. You're not supposed to be smoking. You can have gum, if it helps."

The girl was small for her age. Undernourished, the detective thought. A social worker sat beside her. A tape recorder whirred, recording everything that was said.

"We've been sitting here for half an hour, Sharon. Are you going to tell us

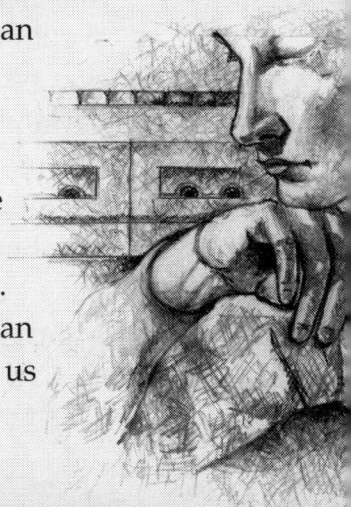

what happened? We know you stole the stuff. The shopkeeper identified you. You're wasting our time."

Sharon said, "Give us the gum."

The detective handed her the gum.

"Cigarettes are bad for your health."

"Yeah. Like I care about that."

Sharon popped the gum in her mouth and spoke. "Like I said, my scumbag dad took off. Mum was hopeless. She was doped out of her brain or drunk most of the time. I don't know how we got by. When I was about six my brother was born. I have no idea who his scumbag father is. There was never any money. I went to school sometimes but not when it was cold. I didn't have a jumper. Well, not until I nicked one. I nicked one for my brother too. They were in someone's yard, drying. It was a posh house. They wouldn't miss a couple of jumpers. That was when I was about eight. Mum didn't say anything. I don't think she even noticed. Then I started pinching stuff from the milk bar. Lollies mostly, but I was hungry. I stole bread sometimes. And baked beans. I hate baked beans but Mum never cooked. I knew it was against the law but no-one helped us."

The detective leaned forward. "Is this meant to make me cry Sharon? Just drop the sob story and tell us about the CDs. Or were you planning on eating those too?"

Sharon looked at the detective. He was a big man. He looked like he hadn't shaved for a few days, but it was probably just a few hours. He had a bit of a gut. He looked mean. Mean and bored. The last thing he wanted was to be stuck in a room with a 13-year-old street kid, chasing a few hundred dollars worth of CDs. He'd heard it all before. Sharon and he were on the same merry-go-round.

"I'd like to throw the book at you," he said.

Sharon popped the gum at him.

"It'd make your job easy if I just confessed, wouldn't it? You'd like that."

"We don't need a confession. We've a witness. We've the CDs."

Sharon thought for a moment.

"Yeah, well. I'm afraid I can't help you, mate. I've never seen those CDs before. I've no idea how they got into that bag. It's not even my bag. Sorry."

The detective sighed. It was going to be a long night.

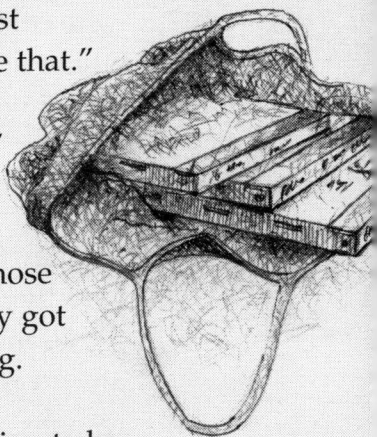

end

WHAT IS A CRIME? This seems like a simple question. Doesn't it? Is crime simply an act that breaks the criminal laws? Can you break the law but not be found guilty of committing a crime? We all think we have a good idea about what is right and what is wrong.

Borrowing money is okay, but stealing it is a crime. Killing someone deliberately is a crime. Or is it? What about a soldier at war?

In the story, Sharon has admitted to a series of crimes. If she is telling the truth, she is guilty of theft. But she was in a desperate situation. She was looking after her brother. If you were cold and poor and alone, what would you do? If you were the judge would you find Sharon guilty of a crime?

crime:

an act that is punishable by law. We also say some shameful acts are crimes even though they might not be illegal.

Murder? That's your problem

Murder, theft and assault are crimes dealt with by the police and the courts. But these, and many other crimes, were not always treated as crimes that society was responsible for punishing. They were once considered, by many societies, to be a personal matter between the victim and the wrongdoer. It was up to the individual, perhaps with the help of his family and friends, to take revenge. This was usually in the form of taking an eye for an eye or a tooth for a tooth. The legal name for this is *lex talionis*—the code of revenge.

Revenge wasn't just taken on people. If an animal injured a person, the animal would be wounded or killed. Sometimes an object was punished. If a rock killed someone, well, it had to be dealt with. It might be destroyed, or, as happened in ancient Greece, it might be banished.

Is revenge a good idea?

Revenge might satisfy the individual, but it leads to problems for society. It never ends; one crime leads to another. As soon as revenge is taken, those who have suffered then wish for revenge in turn. This leads to long-running blood feuds and many innocent people suffering. Often under *lex talionis* the strongest people just did as they liked, knowing that no-one was able to take revenge. Might was often seen to be right. People were not safe to grow food and lead

The Texas Rangers were a police force started in 1835. They never gave up the chase until they had caught the suspect.

useful lives in peace—and everybody suffered.

To stop the damage that a code of revenge wreaked on society, rules were established about how wrongdoers could be dealt with. If a person had been deliberately wounded by someone, the guilty person would have to suffer the same wound in return.

The idea was to punish, not to kill. For an assault, for example, the person inflicting the punishment would not be allowed to kill the guilty person. If this happened, the punisher would have to be killed as well. The punishment had to match the crime. The idea was to remove the anger created by the wrongdoing and to restore harmony in the community.

In a society that hunted with spears a wrongdoer might have had to stand in one place and have spears thrown at him. He could duck and weave, but honour would not be satisfied until he had been speared in the thigh.

As cities became larger it was no longer possible to rely on revenge for justice. What would happen at peak hour if there were no road rules?

Compensation

Many societies used a system of compensation to right wrongs. The wrongdoer had to pay money or give food, goods or animals to the person who had been harmed. There are records that show detailed accounts of what is suitable compensation for a whole range of crimes.

This idea still survives in the justice system today. In Australia, the government pays victims of crimes a certain amount of money as compensation for what they have suffered. In the United States, a guilty person can be made to pay.

> In many Westerns, the hero and the villain settle their differences by shooting it out in the main street, often at high noon. This form of the code of revenge is called frontier justice.

O. J. Simpson. Not guilty one day, $25 million damages the next

In the United States, the family of a murdered person can claim financial compensation from the murderer. The most famous example of this in recent years was the case of O. J. Simpson. Simpson, a football hero and successful actor, was accused of killing his wife, Nicole, and a young man, Ron Goldman. He was found not guilty in a criminal trial.

The families of the victims were not

> **values:**
>
> *qualities which people feel are worthwhile, such as honesty.*

happy with this verdict. They believed that the evidence was very strong that Simpson was in fact the murderer. Ron Goldman's family decided to sue him in a civil court.

The rules in this court are different from the rules in a criminal court. A jury can decide that, based on the evidence, a person probably is guilty.

In this case the jury decided that O. J. Simpson was the most likely person to have committed the double murder. They awarded Ron Goldman's family $8.5 million in compensation, plus $25 million in damages. Simpson has to pay this money. He may be free, but he's no longer rich.

When laws are written down, they are called statutes. There are many statutes covering all areas of life.

Written laws

As people settled in villages, and villages grew into towns and towns grew into cities, societies became more and more complex. It became necessary to write down the rules, or laws, a community lived by. This way everybody could be treated the same, everybody could know what was thought to be right and what

civil court:
court that deals with arguments between people rather than with crimes.

was wrong, and what the punishment for a crime was.

These laws became the responsibility of the government—the particular people who control and administer a society. And it was the government which was responsible for punishing crimes.

In a criminal case the action is brought by the government not the individual. It is the police and the justice system which decide who is to be charged with a crime—not the people who feel they have been wronged. This helped to solve the problems created by *lex talionis*. It wasn't individuals but the government that took revenge on wrongdoers—and the penalties were often very severe. In England, until the end of the 18th century, the death penalty could be given for over 200 crimes.

Police have not always existed. In earlier times the military were used to enforce the law.

Poverty leads to crime

It is difficult for us to imagine what life was like for people even a couple of hundred years ago. Most of us are used to living in places that are safe and where there is a police force to help us if we're in trouble.

In Charles Dickens's novel *Oliver Twist*, gangs of boys in 19th century London were trained as pickpockets and thieves by the villain Fagin.

Conditions in England, for example, in the 18th and early 19th century were appalling. Going to school was a luxury. Food was scarce. Cities were crowded, violent places. The streets were dark and there were many gangs. Robbery and murder were common. There was no police force. Though punishments for even minor crimes were harsh, there was a lot of criminal activity. In 18th century England, stealing a fish might get you hanged. People were often forced, though, to steal and cheat simply to live.

Murder is always a crime, isn't it?

Unfortunately it's not that simple. There is no such thing as a typical criminal and there is no such thing as a typical crime. Every case is different.

How would you judge the following incident if you were on a jury? A man is brought before the court charged with the murder of his wife. He had hit her on the head with a bottle and a heavy stick. He did this quite violently and his wife died as a result of her injuries.

Straightforward? A clear case of murder? No. You need more information. As with Sharon's situation in the opening story, the more we know the more we understand how complex the reasons for committing a crime can be.

> **manslaughter:** *the accidental killing of a person. (You can be sent to prison for manslaughter but the sentence will not be as severe as for murder.)*

Courts try to take into account the cultural backgrounds and religious beliefs of people brought before them. In this case, the man was a tribal member of the Pitjantjatjara people in Central Australia. He lived according to their rules and religious beliefs. One night his wife had begun to reveal tribal secrets. He tried to stop her but she continued to say things that outsiders weren't allowed to hear. It seemed to him at the time that the only way to stop her was to knock her unconscious. What she was doing was a threat to the whole tribal community. It was his responsibility to stop his wife.

What would you do? Put aside his cultural beliefs and apply the law to its fullest? The judge decided that the man had been provoked and accepted a plea of manslaughter. He was not sent to prison, but handed to the tribal elders.

chapter 2

Unsolved Crimes and famous villains

Imagine...

JOEL MITTER WAS IN THE ROOM when the man was murdered. He had been watching a documentary on lions and he had fallen asleep. He didn't actually watch television, in the strict sense of the word, because he was blind. He had been born blind and during his twelve years he had grown accustomed to the fact. He'd never known anything different.

His mother had been careful to raise Joel without pampering him. She wanted him to be independent. His father had left when Joel was six.

On the night of the murder, Joel was annoyed because he was being babysat. The babysitter was his Aunty Jo's boyfriend George Peters. Mrs Mitter had

Joel hurried towards where the sounds had come from. He fell over a chair. It shouldn't have been there. Joel knew where all the furniture was. His foot hit something soft. He bent down and felt the wool of a jumper. There was something on it which was warm and sticky. When he touched the handle of a knife he pulled his hand away. He felt higher up and his fingers settled on a face. It was a man's face. The skin was prickly as if he hadn't shaved.

Joel let out a scream and ran to the door and down the street to where his mother was visiting his aunt.

The police quickly determined that the weapon was a knife from the Mitter's kitchen. They interviewed Joel but he could tell them little. He had fallen asleep. He woke to a sound and that was all.

Joel knew the police suspected him. After all, he had blood on his hands. They suspected his mother and Aunty Jo too, but they both had an alibi. They were angry with his mother and with his aunt because they had rushed to the living room and they had tried to revive George. They each ended up spattered

PEOPLE ARE FASCINATED by crime, both real and imaginary. It is the subject of hundreds of books, films, plays and television shows. Two aspects of crime particularly seem to fascinate people: crimes that have never been solved and famous villains.

In Joel's story all the evidence seems to point to Aunt Jo. What would her motive have been? We'll never know. The interesting thing about unsolved crimes is that there is always vital information which we don't have. Trying to solve a crime is like trying to complete a difficult jigsaw puzzle.

Who was Jack the Ripper?

Charles Dickens, the famous English novelist, died before he completed *The Mystery of Edwin Drood*. No-one will ever know how it was meant to end.

If the number of books written about a case are any indication, then the greatest unsolved crime of all time is the series of murders committed by the person known as Jack the Ripper.

On the night of 6 August 1888, a woman was stabbed more than 39 times in the East End of London. Jack the Ripper had struck for the first time. Twenty-four days later another woman was brutally murdered in the same area. Eight days after that another woman was found murdered and cut with a surgeon's skill. Why didn't anyone see the murderer? He must have been covered in blood.

Women in London were terrified. The Ripper's next victims were two women he murdered on the same night. On 9 November, the last victim fell to the Ripper. After this the murders stopped. No-one knows why. Perhaps the Ripper died. His identity has remained a mystery. Was he a mad surgeon? Or a crazed policeman? Or was he, as some people have suggested, a member of the royal family?

Cyber crime

The information technology revolution has created irresistible opportunities for criminals. Cyber crimes are difficult to solve—and sometimes difficult to define. Computer hackers can transfer funds from one account to another, or they can steal telecommunication services. That is, they can use mobile phones or the Internet, or any other electronic

The World Wide Web and the Internet have made some crimes very difficult to detect.

services, without paying. Cyber crime is difficult to track down and to catch the criminals it is necessary to have international cooperation among police forces.

One of the real problems here is that not everyone agrees about what a crime in cyberspace actually is. For example, there is a lot of material on the Internet that is considered criminal in some places but not in others. Salman Rushdie, a writer, was sentenced to death by an Islamic court after he published a book that offended Muslims. He had to go into hiding. Parts of that book are up on the Net. Should non-Islamic countries help bring Rushdie before an Islamic court even though they do not believe that he has committed a crime?

Sometimes crimes in the digital age are actually committed against the machines which we have come to depend upon. There are many cases of Automatic Teller Machines being stolen. The whole machine is taken out of the wall. They contain a lot of money.

Edgar Allan Poe wrote the first modern detective story, in 1841. It is called *The Murders in the Rue Morgue*. Another of his detective stories, *The Mystery of Marie Roget*, tells of the murder of a young woman. Some people believe that Poe committed the murder upon which his story is based.

Can you solve this mystery?

Here is a great mystery. It would make a great movie—and it's true! In 1889 the Great Exhibition was drawing crowds from all over the world to Paris. An English mother and her daughter booked two rooms at an expensive hotel. Unfortunately the mother fell ill. The hotel doctor said she needed a special medicine.

The daughter went in search of the medicine. Four hours passed before she returned. She was eager to take the medicine to her mother but she was told by the manager that there was no record of her mother ever having been at the hotel. "You arrived here alone," he said. The daughter, confused, said both their names were in the registration book. The manager showed her the book, but only her name appeared. Even though she had watched her mother sign, there was now a stranger's signature above her own.

"She's in room 342," she said.

"No madam. There is a French family staying in 342."

Interpol is an international organisation set up to help police combat international crime. Its members are not police officers. They have no powers of arrest.

She met the doctor but he denied knowledge of her mother. The girl thought she was going mad. No-one believed her. In fact, she spent time in an asylum when she returned to England.

What happened? One theory is that the mother, who had travelled from India, had caught the plague. The hotel doctor was afraid that people would panic. He covered it up, with the help of the hotel. What happened to the body?

Bonnie and Clyde

If you're still in need
Of something to read
Here's the story of Bonnie and Clyde.

Now Bonnie and Clyde are the Barrow gang
I'm sure you all have read
How they rob and steal
And those who squeal
Are usually found dying or dead.

Some day they'll go down together;
They'll bury them side by side;
To few it'll be grief—
To the law a relief—
But it's death for Bonnie and Clyde.

Bonnie Parker 1934

The story of Bonnie and Clyde has been told in song, in films and in books. In the 1930s their crimes were splashed across the front pages of American newspapers.

Bonnie Parker was 19 years old in 1930 when she met Clyde Barrow. He was 21. Soon after meeting Bonnie, Clyde was arrested for burglary and sent to prison. Bonnie helped him escape but he was recaptured. To avoid doing hard labour he convinced a fellow prisoner to cut off two of his toes for him with an axe.

Clyde was released in 1932 and joined up with Bonnie. They began the two-year crime spree that would make them infamous.

They formed a gang with three other people and pulled off a series of robberies in small American towns. There were several close calls but they always managed to shoot their way out of trouble and get away.

Breakout

In January 1934, Bonnie and Clyde helped five prisoners escape from a prison farm in Texas. One of the escapees was a man named Henry Methvin. It was

In 1990, in a town in California, a woman got a terrible fright when she got out of bed in the middle of the night. She stepped on a drunken burglar who had fallen asleep on her rug.

their friendship with Methvin which would cost Bonnie and Clyde their lives.

After the breakout, Bonnie and Clyde continued to commit terrible crimes. They killed two policemen on 1 April 1934, and five days later killed another policeman in Oklahoma. In all, they were suspected of having committed 13 murders.

FBI agents knew where the Methvin family lived and they suspected that Bonnie and Clyde were visiting that house from time to time. The agents had been told that Bonnie and Clyde had held a party on 21 May 1934 at the Methvin house. They were also given a tip-off that Bonnie and Clyde were going to return two days later.

The FBI (Federal Bureau of Investigation) is the famous federal law enforcement agency in the US. The Bureau is responsible for crimes that cross U.S. state borders.

Police set up an ambush on the road they would have to take. Early on 23 May 1934, Bonnie and Clyde's car came into view. The police stepped into the road and opened fire with machine guns. Bonnie and Clyde died in a hail of bullets.

The biggest gangster of them all

Al Capone is one of the most famous names in American criminal history. He was a gangster who rose to power in Chicago in the 1920s. He was born in New York in 1899 and had little education.

In 1920 Capone moved to Chicago and joined a mob of gangsters who were involved in illegal rackets making and selling liquor. This was the era of prohibition.

By 1925, Capone had become the head of a large and feared gang of mobsters. He was ruthless. The famous St Valentine's Day Massacre on 14 February 1929 is believed to have been organised by Capone. On that day, seven members of a rival gang were lined up against a wall in a garage and machine gunned by men disguised as police officers.

The police found it difficult to pin anything on Capone. He was finally sent to gaol for a long stretch on a charge of not paying his taxes. He was sentenced in 1931 to 11 years.

> Prohibition was a period in American history when the sale of alcohol was forbidden. Prohibition gave gangsters the perfect opportunity to make lots of money by selling alcohol illegally.

He served seven and a half years of this, some of it at the notorious Alcatraz prison. When he was released he had lost his mind. He lived quietly with his wife until his death in 1947.

Ned Kelly—hero or villain?

The image of Ned Kelly in his home-made suit of armour is well known in Australia. The story of the Kelly Gang captured the imagination of Australians and many people believe that he was not a criminal but a victim of a terrible system which exploited the poor.

Edward (Ned) Kelly was born in June 1855, in the state of Victoria. His family was Irish and poor and often in trouble with the police. Ned went to gaol for the first time when he was only 16. His mother was arrested for the attempted murder of a policemen, although there was no real evidence that this happened.

Some people regard Ned Kelly as a hero worthy of having a statue of him erected. Others see him as a killer and criminal.

Revenge

Ned wanted revenge. This is why people find his case fascinating. They believe that all his actions were the result of being a victim of authority. He was an underdog and we like to support the underdog.

With his brother Dan and two others, Ned formed the Kelly Gang. In October 1879, four policeman came looking for the Gang. Ned killed three of them. They were now notorious outlaws and 200 police were sent to find them. The Gang robbed banks in small towns and a reward of £8000 was offered for their capture. This was a fortune. At this time a man's weekly wage was only £3.

In June 1880 the Kelly Gang captured the railway station and hotel at Glenrowan. They thought they were safe because the telegraph wire had been cut but a message had got through. A train load of police set out from Melbourne. When the Gang heard the train whistle, they knew they were trapped. They put on the rough and heavy armour they had made out of farm equipment.

At 3.00 a.m., the Gang came out firing. Ned was wounded but escaped into the bush. The rest of the Gang went back into the hotel.

A death mask is a plaster cast taken of the face of a dead person. Death masks were made of prisoners who were executed. They were also made of famous people.

Ned Kelly's death mask.

Ned came out of the bush at 7.00 a.m. and was shot in the legs and captured. The police then set fire to the hotel. The Gang members inside were burnt to death.

Ned Kelly was sentenced to death and hanged at the Old Melbourne Gaol on 11 November 1880. He was only 25 years old. His last words are said to have been "Such is life."

Jesse James—hero or murderer?

There have been many books written and many movies made about Jesse James. He is one of America's most famous bank and train robbers. Like Ned Kelly, a legend has grown up around him. He was a Confederate guerrilla in the American Civil War in the 1850s, and some people say it was the cruel treatment by Union soldiers that turned Jesse to a life of crime.

The first private detective agency in the United States was set up by a Scotsman, Allan Pinkerton, in 1850.

Also like Ned Kelly he is a moral paradox. He was a good father and a strong family man who was shot dead at home while dusting and straightening a picture. His father was a Baptist minister and Jesse held his own religious beliefs. He was also a thief and a killer. Some people believe that he gave part of the money he stole to the poor.

Jesse James was born in 1847. When he was in his early 20s he formed a gang with his brother Frank and their cousins. They held up banks, stagecoaches and trains. Soon they were notorious and feared.

By 1871, the owners of the banks had had enough and the Pinkerton National Detective Agency was hired to track Jesse James down. When a bomb was thrown into his mother's house some people claimed that it was a detective who had thrown it. His mother was injured.

In the end it was greed which destroyed Jesse James. A reward of $5000 had been offered for his and Frank's capture. One of his own gang members thought that if he killed Jesse, he would collect the reward. He shot Jesse James dead on 3 April 1882 at St Joseph, Missouri.

chapter 3
The art and science of detection

Imagine...

Lucy Cardew sat in the back corner of the village hall, trying to make herself as small as possible. She was afraid, even though the hall was filled with people. She wasn't afraid of any of them. She wasn't even afraid of the man at the front of the hall. He was a stranger to her and a man of some wealth. He wore robes trimmed with fur. No-one in her village wore such expensive garments.

It was the witches Lucy was afraid of. Soon they would be brought before these people and tried by the judge who wore fur. Lucy was afraid of the witches because she had heard what they had done to Thomas Winston's young daughters. They were Lucy's age, barely twelve, and they had been much tortured by the women whose very lives were on trial that day. It was the twelfth day of October, 1665, and witchcraft had been uncovered in the small English village of Lutton.

The air was cold, colder than any day that year.

"The Devil has breathed in all the warmth," one woman said.

"Only witchcraft could make an October day so bitter," said another.

The judge called for silence and demanded that the accused women be brought before him. The doors of the hall opened and the two women, manacled, their feet bare, their clothes thin and torn, were ushered in between two men. Lucy stole a glance at them, terrified that if they caught her eye she would be possessed. She was startled. She had no clear idea what a witch might look like, but she did not expect that agents of the Devil would appear so weak, hungry and cold. She knew one of them. It was a woman named Margaret who had sometimes been in Lucy's house. Margaret's eyes were red and swollen and her skin was blue with the cold. How could this be?

The judges's voice boomed out.

"Thomas Winston! Come forward and make your accusation."

Thomas Winston stood up and approached the judge.

"You accuse these women of bewitching your children. Be careful Thomas Winston that you tell the truth. Witchcraft is the most serious of crimes and carries a penalty of death." The judge turned to the women. "If you are witches," he cried out, "we will find you out!"

Thomas Winston began his story.

"The woman named Margaret was employed by me as a nursemaid for my children. I did not find her satisfactory and dismissed her. Soon after, my daughters were wracked by great pains. Bent double with it they were. They cursed and uttered animal sounds."

The hall was silent. People hung on his every word.

"Then in one violent spasm they brought forth from their stomachs these objects and they cried out the names of the accused."

He produced from his pocket a
quantity of pins and nails and coins. He
put them before the judge. The people
gaped.

"Here," he said. "Here is my proof. I
need no other."

"You may need no other," said the
judge, "but this court requires more. I
have called the physician Andrew
Addison. His skills are well known and
he is well acquainted with the ways of
the Devil."

Andrew Addison, a stern, grey-haired
man, stepped forward. He picked up the
objects and turned them over in his hand.

"The Devil has a gift for cruelty," he
said. "I have seen such objects vomited
from the stomachs of bewitched children
before." He turned his gaze upon the
trembling women. "And I have seen how
pathetic the Devil's servants appear when
trapped with all their sins before them.
Do not be fooled by the tears of these
women. They are false."

Lucy did not attend the burning, which
took place the following day in the
village square.

end

THE BURNING of the women in the imaginary village of Lutton was not an unusual occurrence in Europe at the time of the great witch hunts. Between 1484 and 1782 it has been estimated that more than 300,000 women were accused of witchcraft and executed. As illustrated in the story, it was not difficult to prove someone was a witch. The rules of evidence relied very heavily on superstition. A mole or a birthmark or a scar might be enough to raise suspicion. Gossip was accepted as evidence as was the testimony of children. Can you imagine how frightening it must have been to know that no-one was safe?

Once a person had been accused there were certain proofs that could be undertaken. One of these proofs was a cruel torture that almost always resulted in the victim being drowned. A woman accused of being a witch was tied up, taken to a deep pool and thrown in. If she sank and drowned she was considered to have been innocent. If she floated and survived, she was obviously being protected by the Devil. She was then executed, often by being burnt alive.

Witches are said to have familiars. Familiars are spirits who take the shape of animals. Black cats are said to be favourite familiars for witches.

The Salem Witches

Perhaps the best known case of witch-hunt hysteria occurred in the town of Salem in Massachusetts, in the USA. In 1692, four young girls began to behave very strangely. They barked like dogs, or seemed to have been struck blind.

A doctor who was called came away believing that they had been bewitched and that the person responsible was a servant named Goody Glover. Goody Glover had lost her temper with the oldest of the girls not long before the strange behaviour started. If it was revenge they were after, they succeeded. Goody Glover was found guilty and executed.

Although the girls stopped their odd behaviour after Goody Glover's execution, witch fever had struck the community. Accusations of witchcraft were made against many people. Soon the jails were full. Accusing someone of being a witch was a good way of settling a grudge.

In the course of a year, in an atmosphere of fear, 19 innocent

In Germany in the late 16th century, a witch-hunter named Peter Binsfeld is said to have found 6500 men, women and children guilty of witchcraft. All were executed.

men and women were hanged as witches. Another 150 were imprisoned. The witch-hunt ended in 1693 and those who had survived prison were freed.

Have we always agreed on what is or is not evidence?

The fact that witchcraft was even considered a crime, let alone that it was a crime worthy of execution, seems extraordinary to us.

What is just as extraordinary is the way evidence to prove witchcraft was gathered. It wasn't evidence at all. Rumour, torture and superstition were enough for a conviction.

Science has played a major role in modern standards of evidence.

Whatever our changing attitude to crimes, one thing has remained consistent—our desire to solve them and our desire to see the criminal brought to justice.

The ways in which crimes are solved has changed dramatically over time. Today, the proofs offered by Thomas Winston in the story would be thrown out of court. Science and refinements in the art of detection now play major roles.

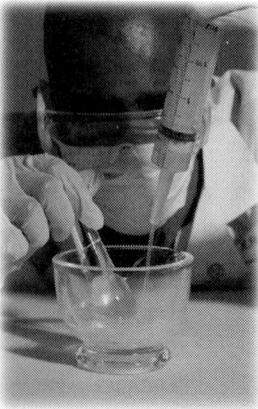

Does it matter how we get proof?

Before science could provide courts with authentic proof of a person's guilt or innocence, evidence had to be obtained in other ways. If there were no witnesses to a crime and no strong evidence linking a suspect to the deed, the best proof of guilt was a full confession. The laws of some countries allowed suspects to be tortured until they had confessed.

The tortures were hideous. Often people confessed to crimes they hadn't committed to put an end to their suffering. Of course, once they had confessed their fate was sealed and they were tortured further as punishment, or executed. In most countries today confessions that are obtained under duress (that is, confessions that are forced out of people) are not admitted in court.

There are thousands of hideous tortures but perhaps the best known is the rack. A person was stretched on the rack until his limbs were torn from their sockets.

Trial by ordeal

It was sometimes the case that a person could prove his or her innocence by undergoing a cruel, physical test. The Saxons in England, for example, would force an accused person to take hold of a

Ordeal by water required a person to plunge a hand into a pot of boiling water and retrieve a stone at the bottom of it. It was thought an innocent person would not suffer any injury.

red hot iron. Of course the resulting injury would be considerable. If the wound healed within three days, innocence was proved. The Saxons believed that God would heal the wounds of the innocent. There were many ordeals a person might undergo. All of them resulted in severe injury.

After the Norman Conquest of England in 1066 it became more common for disputes to be settled in combat. It was believed that God would grant victory to the person who was in the right.

How did methods of solving crime change?

For hundreds of years science and superstition competed in the investigation of crimes. As early as 1248, in China, observations of the effect of drowning on the lungs and the physical signs of strangulation, had been written down. These observations were intended to help in the solving of crimes. The book, *The Washing Away Of Wrongs*,

detective:

a person whose job it is to solve crimes by finding evidence and linking it to the person suspected of committing the crime.

is thought to be the earliest known work which tried to use medical observations as a means of solving crimes.

It took a long time for Europeans to catch up to the Chinese. It wasn't until the 17th century that criminal investigators began to use the increasingly reliable knowledge of doctors to help them. By the late 18th century there were several books available on police medicine.

A ballistics expert can see the differences in bullets fired from different guns. Each gun barrel will leave its own particular marks on a bullet.

Who killed Edward Culshaw?

John Toms was the chief suspect in the murder of Edward Culshaw in Lancaster, England, in 1784. Culshaw had been shot dead, but how could investigators prove that the shot came from Toms's pistol? In those days there was no equipment to run ballistic tests. However, in 1784 guns were loaded by pushing gunpowder down the barrel, then packing this into place with a piece of cloth or paper. The lead ball was then rammed down the barrel, followed by another piece of cloth or paper. The gun was then fired and the process repeated for the next

ballistics: the study of firearms.

shot. John Toms had used a piece of paper which had a poem printed on it. He had put the rest of the paper in his pocket. When Culshaw's head wound was examined, the torn piece of paper was recovered. When the blood had been cleaned from it, it was found to match the paper in Toms's pocket. This evidence was presented in court and Toms was convicted of murder on the strength of it. This is one of the earliest recorded cases of evidence of a scientific nature being used to win a conviction.

Poison—The invisible killer

Poisons are chemicals which can harm people.

Violent murders often left telltale evidence of the killer. Even without the benefit of modern forensic methods, general observation could often point to the guilty person. Poison, however, offered an undetectable and unprovable method of killing the victim. For hundreds of years the world's favourite poison was arsenic. It was first made in the 700s by an Arab alchemist. Because it had no taste and no smell it was easy to slip it into a drink or into food.

The effects of arsenic were dramatic. The victim would vomit, be crippled by stomach pains and die. The symptoms looked like those of cholera, a common disease. Even if someone was suspicious, there was no way to prove that the victim hadn't simply died of the disease.

alchemist: *An early type of chemist.*

Can poison be detected easily?

Scientists were interested in finding ways of detecting arsenic and other poisons in the body. A Swedish chemist, Karl Wilhelm Scheele, found a way of detecting arsenic in bodies as early as 1775. However, his method only worked if there was a large quantity of arsenic present. This was not always the case. Other chemists refined his technique until, in 1836, James Marsh, an English chemist, had discovered a way of detecting the poison in tiny quantities.

The ability to detect other poisons improved as well. The pioneering work of the Belgian chemistry professor Jean Servais Stas paved the way for modern toxicology (the study of poisons). Stas had been called in to examine the organs

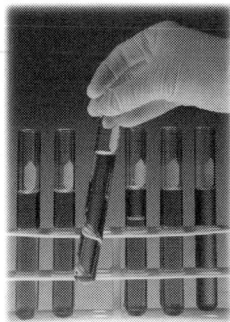

Scientists are able to detect tiny quantities of poison in blood samples.

brand:

a metal shape which is made red hot before it is pressed against the skin.

of a man who police suspected had been murdered. Stas's complex method of isolating poison in the man's tissues led to the conviction of his killer. In this case, the poison was nicotine.

How were criminals identified?

A continuing problem for investigators was the identification of criminals. Police forces kept detailed records of the appearance of known criminals, but appearance was easy to alter. If a man grew a beard, he no longer matched his description. In some societies criminals were branded, even if the crimes they committed were petty. In ancient China, a thief might be branded with a hot iron on his forehead, or he might have his nose sliced off. In other countries, fingers or whole limbs were amputated. These acts were to punish the criminal but also to mark him out from the people he lived among.

After being arrested, people are usually photo-graphed.

COUNTY JAIL

003-954700214

The Bertillon System

Alphonse Bertillon worked in the criminal investigation department of the Paris police force. He thought that there had to be a better method of keeping track of criminals than the descriptions in his department. He devised a system which made it possible to know whether a person who had been arrested had been arrested previously under a different name.

His system involved taking careful measurements of at least fourteen different parts of the body. The measurements were then catalogued and when a criminal was arrested his measurements were checked against the catalogue. This seems clumsy, but once the system had been set up it worked quite well. Criminals who gave false names could now be traced. Bertillon's system was in use in many countries in Europe by the middle of the 1800s.

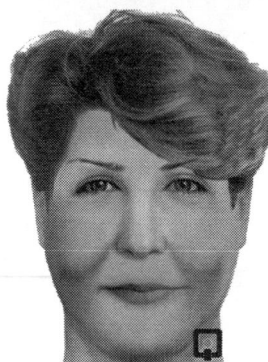

Fingerprints

Bertillon's system was effective but it was inefficient. It wasn't 100 per cent reliable either. It seems obvious to us now, but before the 1800s no-one really paid much

Police use standard components, such as particular types of eyes or ears, to construct identikit pictures of suspects.

attention to the patterns on the tips of our fingers. Certainly no-one suggested that no two people share the same prints. Even identical twins have different prints.

Investigators began to be interested in the possibilities offered by fingerprint identification in the 1880s. The work of Sir Francis Galton, who published his book *Fingerprints* in 1892, showed that a person's fingerprints were unique and therefore they could be used to place that person at a crime scene if a match was found.

Galton's work attracted a lot of attention. In Argentina a man named Juan Vucetiche began collecting and classifying fingerprints. His work led to the first documented case of fingerprints being used to win a conviction for murder.

Murder in Argentina

When two children were found battered to death in the town of Necochea in 1892 in Argentina, an investigation began. The murder of the children horrified the nation. It was front-page news. The investigation went nowhere so an expert investigator was called in to solve the crime. The man chosen was a police inspector named Alvarez. Alvarez knew about Vucetich's research with fingerprints and was interested in it as an investigative method. He searched the crime scene carefully and found a clear print, etched in blood on a door. He actually removed this section of door and took it away with him.

The mother of the children, Francesca Rojas, was a suspect, but there was no proof against her—yet. Alvarez organised for her fingerprints to be taken and when he examined them he found that her thumb print matched the bloody print on the door. She had to have been at the scene of the crime.

She confessed to the murder of her own children. They had become a nuisance because her lover didn't like them.

It is now a matter of police routine to take someone's fingerprints once they have been arrested.

How did fingerprinting become a major tool in crime detection?

The Rojas case led to Argentina being the first country in the world to use fingerprinting as a regular part of police investigative work. Other South American countries soon followed.

The most famous detective in fiction is Sherlock Holmes. The first Holmes story, written by Sir Arthur Conan Doyle, appeared in 1891. Holmes was so popular that when Conan Doyle killed him off in the story *The Final Problem*, there were so many complaints from the public that he had to bring him back to life.

In England Sir Edward R. Henry developed a system of classifying fingerprints and his system was adopted by Scotland Yard. He was appointed head of Scotland Yard in 1901 (Scotland Yard is Great Britain's most important crime investigation organisation).

With the arrival of computers, the classification and checking of fingerprints has become much simpler. Despite the availability of sophisticated identification tests, fingerprints remain an essential part of any investigation.

chapter 4
Forensic science

Imagine...

ROGER PETERSON was not allowed to have a dog or a cat.

"It's pretty lonely being an only child sometimes. A pet would be good company," he said just before his birthday.

His father put down his paper and said with a smile: "I'm glad you've brought this up Roger. We've been concerned about that for quite a while. What about a little girl?"

Roger looked horrified.

"No. You can't. Because you see...because...because I'm allergic to girls."

Roger's father went back to his reading.

"What a shame," he said.

On Roger's birthday he was given a guinea pig. He was ecstatic. He named it Joan.

When Roger learned that the family was to go away for a month, he was excited about the trip, but worried about Joan. Who would look after her? The next-door neighbour promised that her son, Ian, would feed Joan every day and clean out the cage once a week. He was 15 and a responsible boy. Roger's parents would pay him ten dollars a week.

When Roger and his parents came back from their holiday, the first thing Roger did was rush out into the yard to check on Joan. The cage was clean, there was fresh water and fresh carrots and cut grass. Obviously Ian had been in that day. Roger could see Joan's shape in the corner. He called out to her as he opened the cage door. She didn't move. The smell of rotting flesh made him feel ill.

Ian said that Joan must have died overnight. Roger did not believe him. He suspected immediately that Ian had killed her so that he wouldn't have to look after her every day. How could he prove it?

"I can tell you how long the guinea pig's been dead," said Andrea. Andrea was a girl in Roger's class. She was a brain and she had a spider collection.

"Joan's buried," said Roger. "I can't prove anything."

"Well, let's dig her up," said Andrea. "She's only been in the ground for 24 hours. Did you wrap her in anything?"

"A piece of plastic."

"Perfect." Andrea said excitedly. "The maggots will still be on the body."

After school that day Andrea came over to Roger's house. She dug up Joan. From time to time she would pick something off the body and put it into a jar. When she had finished, she put Joan back in the ground and covered her with dirt. She held the jars up for Roger to see. In one of them there were several dry, dark, oval-shaped cases. In the other were two or three wriggling white maggots.

"Gross!" said Roger.

"Yes. But I have an answer for you. Joan has been dead for at least 20 days. You see, Roger. I love blowflies. You should get some meat and leave it somewhere where the flies can get to it. It's fascinating. You can see the whole lifecycle of a blowfly, from egg to larva to pupa to adult."

"I thought lava came out of a volcano."

"Different lava. Different spelling. Listen. The blowfly sniffs out a rotting corpse. No disrespect to Joan. It lays its eggs. A day later the egg develops into the larvae. These are the maggots. They feed until they're big and fat. Their skin hardens into a kind of shell. This is the pupa. Inside the pupa the blowfly develops until it emerges and flies away. Brilliant, isn't it?"

"It's disgusting."

Andrea ignored this.

"So. Here we have some empty pupa cases. That means that one whole lifecycle has been gone through and that takes at least 20 days. I'd say, Roger, that Joan died pretty soon after you left her in Ian's care. You know what that means?"

"He killed her?"

"Probably. He wanted to collect the money and make it look as though he'd done his job right up to the last day."

Roger couldn't wait to tell his parents and he couldn't wait to see the look on Ian's face.

end

DETECTIVES KNOW that whenever a person commits a crime, there will be evidence that will link the criminal to that crime. Sometimes the guilty person is never found. There might be plenty of evidence but the link to a particular person just can't be made. There have been many cases where the police are fairly certain who committed a crime, but they are unable to prove guilt.

Nevertheless, it is true that a person will always leave something at a crime scene or take something away, even if it is only a fibre or a hair.

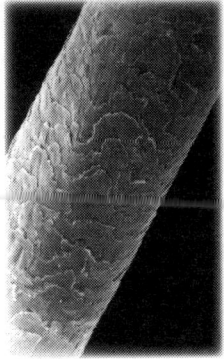

Hairs are pieces of evidence frequently left at a crime scene. Forensic scientists examine them micro-scopically to help reconstruct the crime.

The scene of the crime

When a crime has been committed the first task for the police is to make sure that nothing is moved. Evidence can easily be disturbed or destroyed. The scene is photographed from many angles. The photographs provide an accurate record of the position of evidence. When measurements have been taken of where bits and pieces were found, the evidence is collected for closer examination. Investigators wear gloves and special clothing when

forensic:
relating to crime detection.

In 1910 Professor Edmond Locard worked out his "trace evidence" theory. He said that a criminal will always either take something away from a crime scene or leave something there.

collecting evidence. This protects the evidence from being contaminated.

One of the first jobs for investigators is to dust for fingerprints. A fine dust is brushed over surfaces and it clings to the oils left behind when we touch anything. The print is photographed and then lifted with a piece of sticky tape. If there are tyre tracks or footprints a cast is taken of these.

Evidence is collected by police or other investigators, but in serious crimes such as murder, a forensic scientist will probably attend the scene. The scientist knows precisely what to look for and can tell a lot, for example, by looking at the way blood has sprayed or splashed. In a bomb blast, bomb experts know what is or isn't significant among the rubble.

What might be useful evidence?

Obviously, objects such as guns, or bullets, or bloodstained knives are important pieces of evidence. The forensic scientist is equally interested in much smaller objects such as fibres from clothes, or slivers of glass, pieces of paint, hair, skin, dirt or splinters. Blood or other body fluids provide a large amount of information.

pathologist: *a scientist who specialises in bodily diseases.*

All the evidence is carefully labelled and it is very important that a record is kept of everyone who has contact with it from its collection to its presentation in court. This is called the chain of evidence and if there is doubt about any link in that chain, the evidence might not be accepted by the court.

You probably don't want to know this but...

There are many branches of forensic science. There are scientists who specialise in bullets and firearms, soils, fibres, chemicals and blood. Some forensic scientists are specialists in analysing bodies after death. Their job is to try to establish, through an autopsy, a cause of death by examining the organs.

Could flies help the police solve crimes?

There is one branch of forensic science which doesn't get much publicity— forensic entomology. An entomologist studies insects. A forensic entomologist is

autopsy:

the examination of a body after death. An autopsy is done to establish the cause of death where this is uncertain.

interested in getting information about a murder by examining the insects which have fed on the corpse.

As far as insects are concerned, a dead body is nothing more than a huge piece of meat. When it begins to decay and smell, insects are attracted to it. This can happen quite quickly after death. Forensic entomologists can estimate the time of death because they know the habits of the insects which begin feeding and laying eggs on and in the body. By looking at the life cycle of insects found at the time a body is discovered, it is possible to estimate how long they have been on the corpse. Where a body has been undiscovered for a long time, scientists can still estimate the time of death because insects arrive in predictable patterns. The blowflies come first, followed by creatures which feed on their maggots, followed by beetles and so on. The type of insect present, the age of pupae or larvae, all provide clues as to the time of death.

A psychiatrist in Brazil explained that the reason he shot one of his patients dead was that he was sick and tired of dealing with mad people.

A case with everything

Sometimes identifying a corpse and its time of death can be very complicated and involve many branches of forensic science. In Wales in 1989, a body was dug up in a garden. It was rolled up in carpet and had decomposed to the point where it was really just a skeleton. The socks, bra, panties, sweatshirt and trousers were not yet completely rotted away, and the skeleton still had a full head of blonde hair.

The scientists began the long process of solving the puzzle. They were able to say quickly that this was a female in her late teens, and from the position of the body it was clear that she had been murdered, or at the very least that someone didn't want her found. From the amount of decay that had taken place she had been buried for at least two years, but probably much longer.

A dentist who examined the teeth gave the dead girl's age as fifteen and a half. Forensic scientists were able to show from her clothing that she could not have been buried before 1981. She was wearing a sweatshirt that was not manufactured before

A person can be identified from his or her teeth. If a person has ever visited a dentist there will be a dental record. Everyone's dental record is different.

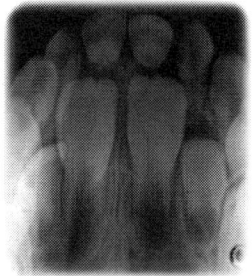

that date. So, the time of her death was being narrowed down to between 1981 and 1987.

Insects again

A forensic entomologist, after examining all the insect evidence, was able to say that the body had been buried for at least five years. Coffin flies, which feed on buried bodies, take three years to strip the flesh from a corpse. The presence of a large colony of woodlice (slaters), which feed on the bones, indicated that a further two years must have passed. It would take them two years to establish so large a colony after the departure of the coffin flies. This now put the death at before 1984.

The garden where the body had been found was behind a pair of houses which had been turned into flats. A person who had lived there in the 1980s recognised the carpet and remembered when it had been laid. This further narrowed the time of death.

Still, police had no idea what the girl looked like or who she was. An expert in forensic

ondontology:
the area of forensic science which deals with teeth.

medicine reconstructed her face, based on her skull and sculpted a clay likeness. A social worker thought she recognised the face. It looked like a 15-year-old girl named Karen Price who had run away from a children's home eight years earlier. With a name, police could check dental records. Karen's dental chart matched the teeth in the skull.

Her identity was finally established using the then new technique of DNA matching. Karen's parents gave blood samples for comparison with DNA material taken from the bones. They matched.

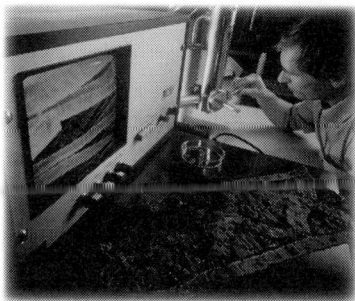

Evidence may be hidden in strange places. Modern technology allows the police to obtain information from all kinds of sources.

The culprits are found

The case of Karen Price's murder was solved when one of the people involved came forward and admitted his part in it. He saw the clay likeness and her name on a television show. He named the murderer, who denied any involvement. However, a girl who had witnessed the murder also came forward and identified both men. Karen had been murdered sometime between July 1981 and May 1982, by a 16-year-old boy and a 21-year-old man. Both were found guilty and sent to jail.

DNA, the newest forensic weapon

Advances in technology now mean that there is really no such thing as a clueless crime scene. Now matter what precautions a criminal takes, something will be left behind, even if it is only a flake of skin, or a hair. This is enough to get a DNA profile.

A piece of skin can be matched to its owner with only a one-in-five-million chance of error. DNA can be used to say with absolute certainty that a particular person did not commit a crime. At the moment though it can't, with absolute certainty, say that a person did.

What it can do is indicate that in all probability a particular person committed a particular crime.

In many parts of the world police are building DNA databases that contain the profiles of known criminals and victims.

In Canada, in 1998, a murder was solved by tracing a pet hair found at the crime scene to the murderer's cat.

Digging up the past

The science of DNA is relatively new, but it is helping to solve crimes that have been unsolved for many years. In the period before DNA technology, blood, body fluids and hair taken from crime scenes were kept in the hope that identification might be made further down the track.

> DNA is short for deoxyribonucleic acid. It provides a kind of genetic fingerprint. Everyone's DNA is different, with the exception of identical twins. It is found in every cell in the body.

The murder of 13-year-old Candice Williams in 1978 wasn't solved until March 1992. In 1978 forensic technology wasn't precise enough to link the body fluids found at the scene to a suspect named Patrick Hassett. With the development of DNA testing, the link was made and Hassett was sentenced to life imprisonment.

DNA can also prove a person's innocence. In 1998 the body of John McInnes was exhumed. He was suspected of having murdered three women in Edinburgh in Scotland in the late 1960s. Body fluids and hair had been found on one of the women's bodies and this evidence had been kept on file. A DNA sample was taken from

> **exhume:** *to dig up.*

McInnes's thigh bone (DNA does not deteriorate after death). If it matched the DNA profile taken from the hair and body fluids, he was guilty. His sister always claimed that he was innocent, but the newspapers assumed that he was guilty and long articles were written which upset the family. The DNA tests proved that John McInnes was innocent.

A single blood cell contains enough information to link a person to a crime scene.

The Fugitive: DNA proves his innocence

One of the most famous criminal trials in America was that of Dr Sam Sheppard. Sam Sheppard was a successful doctor. He was handsome, married and had a seven-year-old son. In 1954 his wife, Marilyn, was beaten to death in her bedroom. Sheppard claimed that he was sleeping downstairs on the couch at the time, when he was awakened by the sound of his wife screaming. He rushed upstairs and met a "bushy-haired man" and struggled with him. He chased the man outside but was knocked unconscious by him.

The police did not believe Sheppard's story. They could find no evidence of a third adult in the house and when it was revealed that Sheppard was having an affair with another woman, they thought they had a motive.

The story of Sam Sheppard captured the public imagination so fully that it became the basis of a successful television series called *The Fugitive*. More recently a movie was made. It was also called *The Fugitive*.

No murder weapon was ever found. A trail of blood was found in the house and it was claimed that this blood had dripped from the murder weapon. The jury accepted this and found Sheppard guilty of murder. He served ten years in prison. The Supreme Court acquitted him of the crime at a second trial much later. The court recognised that he had not had a fair trial the first time.

acquitted: *found not guilty.*

Sheppard always claimed that he was innocent and he never changed his story. After ten years in gaol, he was a broken man. He died an alcoholic in 1970.

In 1997 DNA testing on the blood found at the house proved that it didn't belong to Marilyn or to Sam Sheppard. There had been a third person there, just as Sheppard had said.

chapter 5
Police, lawyers and judges

Imagine...

THERE WERE SIX of them. They called
themselves The Watchers. They called
themselves this because they were all in a
play at school and the play was called *The
Watchers*. There were three boys, all aged
13, and three girls, also aged 13.

The club had started as a kind of joke.
Jenny, whose parents were hardly ever
home, had invited the cast around to her
house after school one day. She lived in a
big house. She had invited the group
around even though the girls would
normally have wanted nothing to do with
the boys, especially Joey Harrap. He was
a real dork. Still, rehearsing at her place
was better than being stuck at school. At
least there was food.

After a couple of rehearsals, the group relaxed with each other. It wasn't so bad having the boys. They decided that it would be cool if they formed a secret society. In Jenny's yard there was a little shed, only it was like a tiny version of a house. It was called a Wendy house. It was perfect for a clubhouse.

"Why do we need to form a secret society?" asked Joey.

The five other members looked at him as if he were nuts. As if you needed a reason to form a secret society.

"Because, dipstick, we have a place to meet and it will be exciting. No-one else will know."

Jenny pricked her finger and squeezed a droplet of blood out.

"I'm not mixing blood," said Joey. "Hepatitis. AIDS."

If looks could kill, Jenny would have been arrested for murder.

They settled for linking fingers and taking an oath.

The Watchers didn't actually do anything. Jenny liked the name because she thought it sounded like they were always on the alert for crime. They met in the Wendy house and ate lollies mostly.

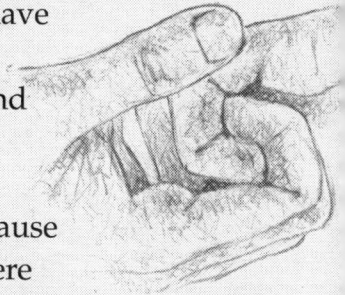

They never actually came across anybody committing a crime. They were a little surprised by this because in *The Secret Seven* crimes were always being committed right under that group's nose.

Then there was a crime committed. It wasn't a spectacular crime, but it was definitely a crime. The Watchers had a money box. Every week each member would put two dollars from their pocket money into the box. It wasn't really a box. It was the drawer of a desk. The money was safe there because the Wendy house could be locked. This paid for the lollies. Once they bought coffee because they thought that would be cool, but nobody liked it. It had been Jenny's idea.

One afternoon Jenny called The Watchers together and announced that the money box had been broken into. Five dollars had been stolen and she knew who had done it. They watched her, breathless with excitement.

"The thief," she said, "is in this room."

She looked directly at Joey. He jumped up.

"I did not take that money!" He was outraged.

"I didn't say you did," said Jenny

calmly. "But I guess you have a guilty conscience."

"You took it," said Joey. "And now you're blaming me. How could I get in here? You're the only one with the key."

"You borrowed my key. Remember? You must have had it copied."

The meeting became very noisy. The boys supported Joey. The girls stood by Jenny. They yelled at one another. They were so loud in fact that Jenny's mother came down to the Wendy house and told them all to be quiet.

That was the end of The Watchers. The only time they'd been faced with a crime they'd lost their heads. They didn't have very much to do with each other after that. If they'd bothered to check, they would have found the five dollars squashed up in a corner of the drawer.

end

MOST OF US believe in the idea of justice. We accept that justice is best left to the courts. We don't take the law into our own hands and seek personal revenge for any wrongs that are done to us or to the people we love. In fact, it is against the law to do so. When criminal acts affect us directly it is easy to let our emotions run away with us. If the members of The Watchers had stopped for a moment and thought about what had happened, they might still be friends. What they really needed was an outside person to look at what had happened, examine all the facts and come to a decision. In a way, this is the role of police, lawyers and judges. These people are responsible for investigating, arguing guilt or innocence, interpreting the law and then applying it.

Laws are made so that society can function in harmony. Of course, it is pointless having laws if there is no-one to enforce them. This means that we give certain people the right to make the laws and others the right to enforce them. The police, lawyers and judges all have roles to play in making sure that people who break the law are brought to justice.

In some courts lawyers wear wigs and gowns that echo the clothes of the 18th century.

Were there always police?

The idea of a police force with special powers is relatively new. In many ancient societies it was the military which kept law and order, under the direction of the emperor or king.

In the early days of white settlement of the United States communities were small and the threat of the stocks kept people under control. If a stranger came to town he was noticed immediately. If he was a suspicious character he would be banished to another town. There was no need for a police force in these small communities. Later, when the West was settled and when there were large numbers of people moving through towns, it was the job of the sheriff and his deputies to keep law and order.

In France by the 18th century, there was an established police force, that had extensive power of pursuit and arrest. They didn't need much evidence to arrest a person and they could search houses without permission. Such powers led to innocent people being accused of crimes and being thrown into prison. At the

These days police serve the community in a number of ways, such as directing traffic.

Police shows on television are very popular. The longest running crime show is *Murder She Wrote*, starring Angela Lansbury. It ran for 14 seasons and 264 episodes.

Police investigations may not always take place on land. There is a special branch of police who deal with crimes on the water.

same time the police did manage to make certain areas safer.

To the English, the French system seemed to ignore the rights of individuals. Authorities were reluctant to follow the French example and create a regular, paid police force. The result was that large cities, especially London, were dangerous places to live. They were very dangerous indeed after dark.

There were some people who patrolled the streets, attempting to stop crime. They were either unpaid, or paid poorly and it was easy for criminals to bribe them. It was also easy to bribe the local magistrate.

Enforcing the laws

The streets were so unsafe that a man called Henry Fielding (he was a famous novelist) suggested that the only way to stop crime was to pay special constables a decent wage. They wouldn't take bribes if they didn't have to. His idea was tried out in 1753. His group of men—called the Bow Street Runners because Fielding was a magistrate of Bow Street Court at the time—were the first police force in England. They cleared the streets of gangs in a short time. They weren't well trained though. It wasn't until the Metropolitan Police Force was set up in 1829 by Sir Robert Peel that policing became a profession. English police are still called "Bobbies" after Sir Robert Peel.

A chemical from the capsicum vegetable is used to make a spray police use as a weapon.

The idea of a paid police force was not a popular one. Although it eventually became the model for police forces in many parts of the world, in the beginning people thought the Metropolitan Police Force was a terrible threat to their freedom. Robert Peel said, "I want to teach people that liberty does not consist in having your house robbed by organised gangs of thieves."

Judges and judgements

The way in which in courts operate is different in different parts of the world. Even the role of lawyers differs from place to place. In Europe (but not Great Britain) the code of law evolved from the Roman Law. Wherever Europeans set up

lawyer:

a member of the legal profession who either represents someone in court or prepares the case before it goes to court.

colonies—in Africa, Asia and South America—the legal system they brought with them was the Roman system. In Great Britain and its colonies—Australia and the United States especially —the legal system was based on Common Law. So what is the difference between Common Law and Roman Law (also called Civil Law)?

Under Common Law the decisions made by judges depend on decisions which other judges have made before them in similar cases. Under Roman Law the decisions depend on statutes, which are laws made by the government.

The major difference between them, however, is that under Common Law the person who is accused of a crime is presumed to be innocent. No matter how much how much it looks like a person committed a crime, the court must believe that the person is innocent until proven guilty.

How does the legal system work?

Our system of law is called the adversary system. The case is argued by the lawyers on both sides. It is up to the prosecuting lawyers to prove beyond reasonable doubt that the accused committed the crime. The defence must argue strongly that the accused is not guilty. In some cases the defence might argue that the accused person is insane, or not fully responsible for his actions. It is the lawyers who play the main role in presenting evidence. Whoever can convince the judge, or the jury if there is one, will win the case.

The European system is called the inquisitorial system. Here, the role of the judge is very different. It is the judge who leads the investigation and it is the judge who examines witnesses and the accused. The lawyers are there to help the judge and they can ask questions only when the judge has finished. They need permission to do this. In many cases, lawyers are not even necessary.

In court cases, witnesses are called and they are questioned, or cross examined by lawyers from each side. The prosecution is trying to prove that the person charged is guilty. The defending lawyer is trying to prove that the person is innocent.

Passing sentence

One of the biggest responsibilities judges have is sentencing. It is the judge who must decide what punishment is to be

Julius and Ethel Rosenberg were sent to the electric chair in 1953. They were found guilty of giving information about the atomic bomb to the Russians. They were the first United States civilians to be executed for spying. Many people thought that the sentence was too harsh.

handed down when a person is found guilty of an offence. There are not necessarily specific penalties which a judge must enforce. There is usually a minimum penalty and a maximum penalty for a crime. Judges are expected to make their decisions wisely and without prejudice. However, not all judges feel the same way all the time about offenders. Judges who hand out tough sentences are called "hanging judges", judges who don't are called "soft judges".

If you were a judge, do you think you would treat everyone the same way? What if you were faced with two people who had admitted, in separate incidents, to the theft of $100? The first person who comes before you is neatly dressed and polite. He stole the money from a businessman. The second person is dirty, rude to you, speaks poor English and stole the money from an old lady. Do you hand out the same sentence?

chapter 6
Punishment

Imagine...

O N 12 JULY 1782, in the small town of
Misty in Massachusetts, the word
went out that two men were to suffer in
the pillory that day. The pillories were to
be set up in the square. Thomas Wyatt, a
silversmith of good standing in the town,
told his son that morning that he was to
go with him to the square to see what
came of wrongdoing. James Wyatt, a boy
of 12, was excited by the prospect. He
had never seen men pilloried but he had
heard that it was a great entertainment.

Thomas and his son walked towards
the square. They were joined along the
way by a large number of people, many
of whom carried bags bulging with
vegetables, fruit, pieces of wood and
stones. When they reached the square,
Thomas pushed his way to the front of

the crowd. He wanted his son to get a good view of what happened to people who defied the laws of God and the laws of men.

There was a commotion in the crowd. Two men were roughly hurried to the platform, which had been built, and dragged up onto it. James recognised them both. One was Peter Talbot, a drunkard and a simpleton of about 30 years. The other was known to him only as John. He was slightly older and had a reputation in the village for violence. They were manacled and looked dirty and miserable. A well dressed man addressed the crowd.

"These two criminals are brought here on a charge of burglary. They did enter the house of Eleanor Watts and carried away much of her property. It is right and just that they should suffer the pillory before the citizens of this town."

A roar of approval went up. The top half of each pillory was raised, their shackles were undone, and the men were forced to place their hands and head in the semi-circles on the bottom half. The top was then lowered and secured into place. The men were now trapped, uncomfortably bent over and doubtless cold. The one called Peter watched the crowd through terrified eyes. The other showed only defiance.

One of the men who had guarded the criminals stepped forward and produced from his pocket two long nails. He showed them to the crowd who murmured approval. He approached the man named John and swiftly nailed each of his ears to the board behind. He yowled in pain. The other man did not suffer this cruelty.

When the platform had been cleared of guards, the crowd began jeering and throwing objects at the men. Eleanor Watts was the first to do so. She came close to the pillory and threw a jagged rock at the face of the man named John. The rock had caught him above the eye and he bled a good deal. Someone ran onto the platform and put a stinking, dead rat around his neck.

The most vicious missiles were reserved for John. Stones, rocks and wood rained down upon him until his face was hardly recognisable. When it seemed that he had slipped into unconsciousness a woman mounted the platform carrying a bucket. It contained filthy water from the drains and she poured it over his head to revive him. The crowd cheered. He woke, but only briefly. At the blow of the next stone, he slumped in the pillory.

His body was not removed. Peter Talbot stood being insulted, pelted and laughed at for the next 24 hours. When released he could not straighten up.

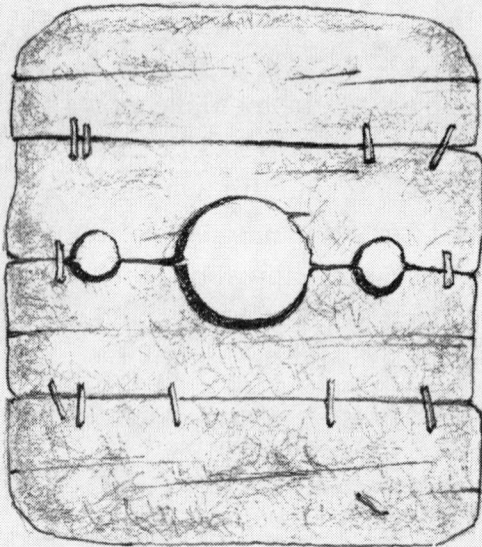

end

THE KIND of public punishment dealt
to Peter Talbot and the man named
John in the story was quite common until
well into the 19th century. Our ideas
about punishment have changed and we
would not consider that such cruelty was
civilised.

However, if the punishment of
criminals were still a public event, do you
think people would turn up? In countries
where hanging is still done in public
huge crowds show up. They don't get as
involved as the crowd in the story, but
they do want to be there to see the
sentence carried out.

Perhaps the best known public
punishments were those involving stocks
and pillories. All over Europe, in the
United States and in Asia, examples of
these structures can be seen. In the stocks,
a person's feet were secured and in a
pillory, the head and hands were secured.

Whenever criminals were confined to
stocks and pillories, a crowd gathered.
The story is not an exaggeration. The
crowd jeered the victim, or threw things
at him or her. It was not uncommon for
people in stocks and pillories to be killed.
Often though they were simply

humiliated and the crowd was able to feel that they had suffered as a result of what they had done.

Who ended up in the stocks and pillories?

People could find themselves punished in the stocks for reasons that seem trivial today. Public drunkenness, petty theft or criticising the authorities could land a person in the stocks or in a pillory. Then they were at the mercy of the mob. If the crowd knew the people being punished and if they liked them, they would survive uninjured. The writer Daniel Defoe (1660–1731), the man who wrote *Robinson Crusoe*, was put in the pillory because of something he wrote about the government. Fortunately many people agreed with what he had written and they brought food for him to eat, rather than to throw at him. He was showered in rose petals instead of filth.

The stocks were used for the last time in England in 1837. The last man to be put in the stocks was Mark Tuck. He was confined to the stocks for drunkenness. Local people arrived in their hundreds to see the sentence carried out.

Things did not always go so well for the people in the stocks. In 1751, a man called Egan and a man called Salmon were charged with highway robbery. They were to be hung for this offence, but this wasn't considered punishment enough, so they were put in the pillory first. If the authorities expected them to survive they were mistaken. The crowd decided that their crime was a serious one. Egan was dead within half an hour and Salmon died of his injuries soon after.

One of the most popular crime writers of all time is Agatha Christie. Her famous detective, Monsieur Hercule Poirot, and her amateur sleuth, Miss Marple, are known to millions.

Why do you think offenders need to be punished?

Over the centuries, people have thought a lot about punishment and produced many theories to justify it. Some have argued that punishment is simply revenge and that this is as it should be. A person who does something wrong must make up for it. Others have said that punishment is really about stopping other people from committing a crime. The public nature of much punishment before the 20th century was designed partly to serve as a warning to people who might be tempted to do wrong. This idea is called deterrence. James Wyatt in the story would think twice before he broke the law, don't you think?

Still other people say that punishment is a way for a guilty person to work out his guilt by suffering as much as his victim. This provided a neat, balanced outcome. In modern times people argue that punishment should be about rehabilitation. Our system of prisons, therefore, should be designed to re-educate inmates and change their values and attitudes.

Can you believe that people actually did these things to others?

Just as ideas about punishment have changed, so too have punishments themselves. You have already read about stocks and pillories, but they are only one of the techniques people have created to inflict suffering.

deter:

to stop someone from doing something by making that person afraid of the consequences.

Punishments fall into two broad categories—capital and corporal. Capital punishments kill the person found guilty of a particular crime. In places today where capital punishment is still allowed by law—this includes many states in the United States—capital punishment is used in only the most extreme of criminal actions, usually murder. In earlier times capital punishment was more widely used and in England, for example, a person might be hanged for robbery.

In ancient Rome, a man of noble birth found guilty of a capital offence would have his head chopped off with a sword. People of lower birth faced being thrown from a place called the Tarpeian Rock. In most parts of the Roman Empire, slaves and thieves were crucified, their bodies left hanging as a warning to others. Crucifixion was quite common in Japan too, where its use continued well into the 19th century.

Hanging and worse

Hanging was frequently used to kill criminals in Europe in the Middle Ages. The structure from which a person hung was called a gibbet. Hanging was reserved for lower-class people. If you were lucky enough to come from a wealthy family but unlucky enough to get caught you

rehabilitate:
to try to make better.

Christians are familiar with crucifixion because Jesus Christ was crucified. The image of Christ on the cross can be seen in many Christian churches.

would probably be beheaded. In some places you would be given the choice of a sword or an axe.

In France, beheading was done with the guillotine. It was named after Joseph Guillotin (1738–1814) and became the official means of capital punishment in France in 1792. Guillotin didn't invent the guillotine but he recommended its use. He thought it a more humane way of executing criminals than beheading them with an axe. It is most often associated with the French Revolution.

The French king, Louis XVI and his wife, Marie Antoinette, were beheaded by the guillotine. It was used until 1981 when France abolished the death penalty. France was not the only country to use a machine like the guillotine. A similar device was used in ancient Persia and in parts of Italy and Scotland.

In England, hanging was considered too good for some criminals. A person convicted of treason—betraying his country—would very likely be hung, drawn and quartered.

capital offence: *offence which carries the death penalty.*

This brutal practice was designed to make the person

suffer as much as possible. First, he was strangled with a rope, but not to the point of death. Then his belly was cut open. The idea was to keep the person alive for as long as possible. If the victim had not died of shock or pain by this time, the final torture finished him off. His body was cut into four pieces—quartered.

In France, the same offence, treason, was punished by attaching the victim to two draught horses and then forcing the powerful beasts to pull in opposite directions. The traitor would be pulled apart.

Charles Dickens's novel, *A Tale of Two Cities*, is set during the French Revolution. The hero, Sydney Carton, goes to the guillotine saying, "It is a far, far better thing that I do, than I have ever done; it is a far, far better rest, that I go to, than I have ever known."

Corporal punishment

Corporal punishment is supposed to be a lesser punishment than capital punishment. The victim is supposed to survive, but this has not always been the case. Corporal punishment is the inflicting of some form of physical abuse on a person. In Medieval Europe people were maimed so that they would always carry the mark of their offence with them.

The last flogging in an Australian prison occurred in 1957, in Melbourne.

They were branded with hot irons or had their tongues cut out, or their ears cut off, or perhaps a limb. They were flogged with the cat-o-nine-tails. Convicts in the early days of white settlement of Australia were frequently lashed with this whip. Often people were flogged until their bones were exposed.

In some societies, offenders were stoned. The list of corporal punishments invented by people is long. Death often followed because of infection of open wounds or loss of blood. In some countries today, corporal punishment is still practised.

Some people call vandalism street art and think that it should be encouraged. What do you think?

Don't vandalise anything when you're in Singapore

In 1993 an American boy named Michael Fay made world headlines when he was sentenced in Singapore to six lashes of the rattan cane. He had pleaded guilty to spray painting cars and to committing other acts of vandalism. These were his first offences. He was also sentenced to four months'

gaol and a $30,000 fine. The rattan cane is designed to hurt. The victim is caned across the buttocks.

How are offenders punished today?

Our attitudes are different today from the attitudes of people hundreds of years ago. At least we like to think they are. There are still some places in the world where limbs are amputated and where prisons are squalid and deadly places.

The role of prisons has changed dramatically. Before the 19th century, prisons were simply places where people were kept before they were tried and before their sentence was carried out. Today, prison is itself the sentence.

It is unusual for a first offender to be sentenced to a gaol term, unless the crime is a very serious one. The preferred consequence for minor offences in many countries is community service. The offender is obliged to perform some sort of unpaid work in the community as a demonstration that he or she is sorry for what they have done.

The cat-o-nine-tails was a vicious whip which took off great quantities of flesh with each lash.

Do some countries still have capital punishment?

Most countries in Europe, many countries in Asia, and Australia, have abolished the death penalty. There remain many places where the death penalty is still lawful. In some countries in Asia the death penalty is applied in cases where drugs have been illegally imported.

Hanging and shooting are the most common methods of capital punishment. There are five countries, all of which follow Islamic Law, where people are beheaded and another seven Islamic countries that allow stoning to death.

In the United States, the death penalty was abolished by the Supreme Court in 1972. It was made lawful again in 1976, in response to the demands of large numbers of voters. Since then almost 500 people have been executed. There are several mechanisms for killing the victim. These include the gas chamber, hanging, the electric chair and lethal injection. Recently there was a great deal of argument over the execution by lethal injection of a woman.

In the state of Texas in February 1998,

Karla Faye Tucker was executed for two murders she had committed in 1983. At the time of the murders she was under the influence of drugs. Since her imprisonment she had become a Christian and had expressed regret for her crimes. This did not save her. She became only the second woman to be executed in America since 1861.

In the United States, the number of people being executed is increasing. In 1991 there were only 19 executions. In 1997, there were 74, most of them in Texas. In 1998 there were 3316 people on death row. Some of these are women.

A final word

When we look back over the history of crime and crime detection, we can see that there have been great developments. Today there is more agreement than there used to be over what is a serious crime and what is not. Our laws are more uniform. There are systems in place which are designed to provide justice. We must also remember, though, that the world

Islamic law: the law as set out in the holy book of Islam—the Koran. Muslims, who follow the teachings of Islam, must obey these laws.

is made up of many different cultures
and not all cultures deal with crimes in
the same way. We must not suppose that
our attitudes and values are the only ones
with merit.

We take so much for granted in modern
life. Our streets are relatively safe. Our
houses are relatively safe. If we become a
victim of a crime we expect that the
police will investigate it. If the guilty
person is found, we expect that the courts
will deal with him or her. I would rather
be living now than in the 18th century.
How about you?

Where to from here?

In recent times there has been an
explosion of books about real crime.
Many of these are gruesome and are not
worth reading. If you check your school
or local library under 364 on the shelves
you will find lots of non-fiction titles.

If you're interested in fiction, the stories
of Sir Arthur Conan Doyle are great. They
are short, easy to read and fascinating.
You can find them in libraries or
bookshops. Stories featuring Nancy Drew
and the Hardy Boys are also entertaining.

You can invite a member of the police
force to come and talk to your class. He
or she will answer all your questions.

Another good idea is to visit a court
while there is a case being heard. You will
see first-hand how the court works.
Check with your parents first and make
sure that the case is an interesting one.

The companion book in the
Phenomena series to this book is *Crime
Night*, by Margaret McAlister. It tells a
story of Ric who thinks of himself as a

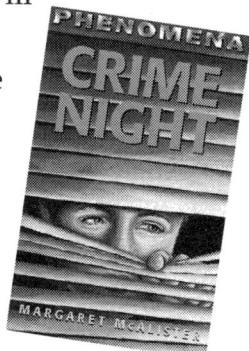

pretty good detective—but he discovers more than he ever really wanted to know. Read it for yourself and decide where fact stops and fiction begins.

Robert's note

I have always loved crime stories. I grew
up reading the Famous Five stories by
Enid Blyton and progressed to Agatha
Christie, Dorothy L. Sayers, Edgar Allan
Poe and Sir Arthur Conan Doyle.
Conan Doyle's stories, featuring
Sherlock Holmes and Dr Watson were
my favourites. I could never guess the
solution to the puzzles, but trying to
was part of the pleasure. That's one of the
great things about mystery stories: in a
way, the reader becomes the detective,
following clues and attempting to solve
the crime before the solution is revealed.
I almost never found the culprit. That's
one reason I never became a detective.
The real reason is that crime in fiction
and crime in real life are two very
different things. I know that I would not
like to examine a real crime scene. I can't
stand the sight of blood for one thing.

I wonder if detectives read detective
fiction? I hope this book has helped you
understand more about the nature of
crime and how we deal with it.

Index